EDGE BOOKS

The Unexplained

HAUNTED HOUSES

by Katherine Krohn

Consultant:
Andrew Nichols, PhD
Executive Director
American Institute of Parapsychology
Gainesville, Florida

Capstone *press*

Mankato, Minnesota

Edge Books are published by Capstone Press,
151 Good Counsel Drive, P.O. Box 669, Mankato, Minnesota 56002.
www.capstonepress.com

Library of Congress Cataloging-in-Publication Data
Krohn, Katherine E.
    Haunted houses / by Katherine Krohn.
    p. cm.—(Edge books. The unexplained)
    Includes bibliographical references and index.
    ISBN-13: 978-0-7368-5450-4 (hardcover)
    ISBN-10: 0-7368-5450-9 (hardcover)
    1. Haunted houses—Juvenile literature. 2. Ghosts—Juvenile literature. I.
Title. II. Series.
BF1475.K76 2006
133.1'22—dc22   2005018487

Summary: Describes the history, experiences, and search for the causes of
haunted houses.

Editorial Credits
Katy Kudela, editor; Juliette Peters, set designer; Kate Opseth and Thomas Emery,
    book designers; Kelly Garvin, photo researcher/photo editor

Photo Credits
AP Photo/Hampton Court Palace, HO, 14
Corbis/Bettmann, 29; Joseph Sohm/Visions of America, 5; Larry Lee Photography, 12;
    Richard T. Nowitz, 25; Robert Holmes, 7
Fortean Picture Library, 17, 18, 27; Janet and Colin Bord, 28; Marina Jackson, 21;
    Roger Brown, cover
Jake Sowers, Phantom Seekers, 23
Mary Evans Picture Library, 6, 11; Peter Underwood, 9, 15

1 2 3 4 5 6 11 10 09 08 07 06

TABLE OF CONTENTS

FEATURES

Chapter 1

WHAT MAKES A HOUSE HAUNTED?

One morning in the early 1980s, gardener Tony Savoy entered one of America's most haunted houses. He planned to water the houseplants on the second floor of the White House. As he climbed the stairs, Savoy didn't notice anything unusual. At the top of the stairs, he flipped on the lights. He saw Abraham Lincoln sitting in a chair. Savoy couldn't believe his eyes. Lincoln had been dead at least 115 years. How could he be sitting calmly in a chair wearing a gray pin-striped suit? Savoy blinked, and Lincoln was gone.

Learn about:
• Abraham Lincoln's ghost
• A ghost in the White House garden
• Unexplained ghostly events

The White House in Washington, D.C.,
is a national landmark. It is also considered
by some to be haunted.

White House Ghosts

Savoy isn't the only person who claims to have seen a ghost in the White House. Other people claim to have seen the ghost of John Adams' wife, Abigail, hanging up laundry. Some say the ghost of James Madison's wife, Dolley, has been seen walking in the White House rose garden. Gardeners once tried to replant the rose garden. But they were scared away when Dolley's ghost told them to leave her roses alone.

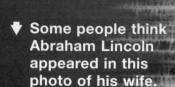

Some people think Abraham Lincoln appeared in this photo of his wife.

EDGE FACT

▲ The Lalaurie House is a famous haunted house in New Orleans. It is also an apartment building.

What Haunts a House?

Many people think of a haunted house as a deserted, old, spooky house. But haunted houses don't have to be empty. Some haunted houses are homes where people still live. Other haunted houses are tourist sites or buildings where people work and visit.

Frequent ghost sightings are just one reason why people think a house is haunted. Sometimes people hear voices or footsteps when no one else is there. Doors may slam shut on their own. Objects may mysteriously fly across rooms. Strange odors with no known source can even drift through a room.

People have been telling ghost stories for hundreds of years. Professional ghost hunters still don't know for sure what haunts houses. This unsolved mystery keeps them wanting to learn more.

▲ Ghostly shadows appeared on a staircase in The Queen's House in Greenwich, England. The tourist didn't notice anything unusual while taking the photo.

Chapter 2

History of Haunted Houses

One of the earliest reports of a haunted house appeared in a letter about 2,000 years ago. People living in a house in Athens, Greece, were scared away by a ghost rattling chains late at night.

The house in Athens stood empty for several years. Then a man named Athenodorus moved into the house. He had heard the ghost stories, but he was curious rather than afraid.

One night, Athenodorus followed the ghost outside. He marked the spot where the ghost vanished. The next day, city officials dug up the spot. They found bones wrapped in chains. After the bones were buried in a new spot, the ghost stopped haunting the house.

Learn about:
- Ancient ghost story
- A haunted palace
- Borley Rectory

Many haunted house stories tell of ghosts appearing late at night.

Ghosts from Long Ago

Edinburgh Castle in Scotland is also a source of many old ghostly tales. Frequent ghost sightings inside the castle and on the castle grounds have turned it into a well-known haunted house. People around the world have heard Edinburgh Castle's ghost stories.

▼ Edinburgh Castle is the scene of many ghost sightings.

EDGE FACT

More than 900 years ago, Edinburgh Castle was the home of kings and queens. The castle was the site of many tragic events. Soldiers died in bloody battles on the castle grounds. Laborers met early deaths while working in the castle.

One of the castle's first ghost sightings happened in 1650. The ghost of a headless drummer boy appeared near the castle. People believe the ghost was trying to warn castle residents of an attack. Later that very same day, an enemy army attacked the castle.

Ghostly activity in the castle includes more than ghost sightings. Workers have heard pipe music from inside the castle walls. They believe a piper, who became lost in the castle tunnels hundreds of years ago, is still trying to find his way out.

Haunted Old England

England's kings and queens have haunted castles throughout much of the country's history. One famous story involves Henry VIII, king of England in the 1500s. The king had six wives. Many of his marriages were unhappy. Two of the king's wives were put to death. The king's gloomy reign is said to have caused the haunting of his home, Hampton Court Palace.

Palace visitors say they have seen a ghost drifting through the courtyard. They claim it is the ghost of the king's third wife, Jane Seymour. She died after their son was born.

Others say they have heard a screaming ghost. They believe it is Catherine Howard, the king's fifth wife. Henry suspected that she was unfaithful to him. In 1542, he ordered her killed.

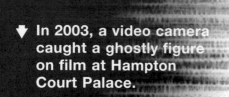

In 2003, a video camera caught a ghostly figure on film at Hampton Court Palace.

Borley Rectory

One of the most haunted houses in England was the home of church leaders. Beginning in the late 1800s, residents began to report strange activities at Borley Rectory. Stories were told of a woman's ghost walking through the rectory's garden. Other people saw a phantom horse and carriage racing in front of the house. Mysterious writings also appeared on the walls.

In 1937, ghost hunter Harry Price moved into the rectory and set up a laboratory. Price saw objects fly through the air. He heard bells ringing that he could not explain. Price searched the building. One day, he found the bones of a young woman buried in the basement. He learned that a nun had been murdered there many years earlier. Price believed the nun's ghost was haunting the rectory.

In 1944, Borley Rectory was torn down. But people still remember it as one of England's most haunted houses.

Borley Rectory in 1892

Chapter 3

HAUNTED HOUSE INVESTIGATIONS

Most people try to stay away from haunted houses. But ghost hunters seek them out. They study haunted places, looking for proof ghosts are present. Many times they find natural reasons for the sights, sounds, and smells that people say are caused by ghosts.

Early Investigators

People began to actively search for ghosts in the 1800s. Members of the Spiritualist Movement believed that spirits of the dead returned to earth as ghosts. They tried to contact these ghosts.

Learn about:
• Spiritualist Movement
• Parapsychologists
• Tools for ghost hunting

In the 1800s, people held séances to try to speak with ghosts.

Some spiritualists truly believed they saw ghosts. Others only pretended. They charged people for séances where they claimed to speak to the spirits of dead loved ones. So many spiritualists were proven as fakes that interest in the Spiritualist Movement faded by the early 1900s.

↟ During a séance, a person called a medium spoke with ghosts. Some mediums tied their hands and feet to prove they weren't playing tricks.

Looking to Science

Meanwhile, in 1882, the Society for Psychical Research formed in England. Members used science to study ghostlike activity.

The society investigated séances and people who claimed to speak to ghosts. Members explained many events as fake. But there were other ghostly sights and sounds that even science could not explain.

Over the years, the society's membership grew. There are now groups in both England and the United States.

Modern Investigators

People are still trying to understand what causes ghostly events. Researchers called parapsychologists believe paranormal activity is one cause. They say a power of the mind called psychokinesis can cause some ghostly activity. People with this ability can use the power of thought to move objects. But they don't always know they have this power.

Some ghost researchers are skeptics. They don't believe in haunted houses. They think hoaxes or natural causes can explain why a house appears to be haunted.

Ghost Hunting Tools

Cameras and video recorders are standard tools for ghost hunters. Photographs and videos can provide proof of ghosts. But many ghostlike images captured on film can be explained by everyday mistakes. A strand of hair blowing in front of a camera lens can make a ghostlike image on a photo. Rain or dust can also be mistaken for a ghost's picture.

Ghost hunters use audio recorders to capture ghostly noises in haunted houses. The human ear alone can't always hear these noises. The recordings often pick up strange sounds thought to be ghosts. These types of recordings are called electronic voice phenomenons (EVPs).

Karen Mossey is a ghost investigator in New Hampshire. She claims to have recorded ghosts of her father, son, and other people. She has taped EVP recordings in her home, in her friends' homes, at haunted houses, and even in her car.

Mossey says the ghosts of both her father and son have communicated with her. On one EVP recording, Mossey says she heard her father tell her he loved her.

Strange ghostlike images can appear in photos. At the time when this photo was taken, the 2-year-old was pointing to the air saying he saw his great-grandmother.

Tracking a Ghost

Special thermometers help ghost hunters check temperatures in haunted houses. The thermometers reveal cold spots in a room. Many ghost researchers believe ghosts can take heat from a room.

Some ghost researchers claim ghosts have an electrical charge. An electromagnetic fluctuation (EMF) reader shows a change in a room's energy field. Researchers claim that unusual EMF readings prove a ghost is present.

Searching for Ghosts

In 2001, ghost hunters Martina and Todd Baker investigated a haunted apartment building in Portland, Oregon. In the 1800s, the building had been a hotel and gambling hall. Underground tunnels connected the building to a river. Kidnappers held men captive in the tunnels and later sold them as slaves to sea captains. Some people believe the spirits of the captive men still haunt the building.

While exploring the basement, Martina felt a slap on her arm. A red mark in the shape of a hand formed on her skin. She then heard a voice yelling at them to get out. As the Bakers hurried upstairs, they heard footsteps chasing them.

Martina and Todd Baker search for ghosts in many places, including schools.

Chapter 4

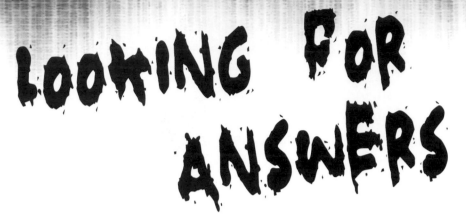

Looking For Answers

Solving the mystery of haunted houses is not easy. Professional ghost hunters rarely find a house that is truly haunted. Drafts can cause cold spots. Wind or leaky pipes can make unusual sounds. Some jokesters have even faked haunted houses to get attention or to scare others. But there are still events in houses that cannot be explained.

Many people do believe ghosts haunt houses. But even this belief leaves people with questions. Why does a ghost seem to stay in a certain house, room, or garden? Ghost hunters have ideas, but no one has absolute proof.

Learn about:
• Answers found in nature
• Why ghosts haunt
• Amityville's haunted house

Tourists hope to catch a glimpse of a ghost at the Winchester Mystery House in San Jose, California.

EDGE FACT

Many Explanations

Over the years, there have been many reasons given for why ghosts haunt houses. Some people believe ghosts have unfinished business to complete on earth. Others believe ghosts want to stay near the people and places they cared about when they were alive.

But not everyone believes ghosts choose to stay on earth. Some think ghosts are trapped on earth. They say people who died a sudden or tragic death may not know they are dead. Their ghosts may haunt the scene of their deaths or return to their former homes. Some ghosts may even appear to be reliving their last moments on earth.

People believe some ghosts return to their homes. In 1891, people claimed the ghostly shadow seated on the left was a past owner of the house.

27

Thousands of people investigate haunted houses. Some researchers want to discover the true causes behind haunted houses. Others try to figure out ways to put an end to ghostly activity. No matter what their reason, ghost hunters will keep trying to solve the mystery.

⬆ Crumbling walls and darkened windows can make people think a house is haunted. But not all spooky houses are haunted.

Amityville Haunting

In December 1975, George and Kathy Lutz moved their family into a house in Amityville, New York. They knew the house had been the scene of a murder a year earlier. But the Lutz family did not feel that the other family's tragedy would have anything to do with them.

A few days after moving in, George and Kathy had second thoughts. They smelled strange odors. They heard doors slamming. The children's beds were moved across the room by an invisible force. The family fled the house in less than a month.

The Lutz's story was first published in *The Amityville Horror: A True Story*. The best-selling book inspired several movies about the house and its haunting activity.

Was the house in Amityville really haunted by spirits of the murdered family? Or did the Lutz family make up the story? New residents in the house never reported ghostly activity. The mystery of this haunted house, like so many others, may never be solved.

GLOSSARY

hoax (HOHKS)—a trick to make people believe something that is not true

paranormal (pa-ruh-NOR-muhl)—something that can't be understood scientifically

parapsychologist (pa-ruh-sye-KOL-uh-jist)—a researcher who studies and investigates haunted houses and paranormal events

psychokinesis (sye-ko-kuh-NEE-sis)—the ability to move objects with the mind

rectory (REK-tuh-ree)—a building where church leaders live

séance (SAY-ahnss)—a meeting to receive the communications of spirits

skeptic (SKEP-tic)—a person who questions things that other people believe in

spirit (SPIHR-it)—the invisible part of a person that contains thoughts and feelings; some people believe the spirit leaves the body after death.

READ MORE

Donkin, Andrew. *Spooky Spinechillers.* Dorling Kindersley Readers. New York: Dorling Kindersley, 2000.

Martin, Michael. *Ghosts.* The Unexplained. Mankato, Minn.: Capstone Press, 2005.

Watkins, Graham. *Ghosts and Poltergeists.* Unsolved Mysteries. New York: Rosen, 2002.

FactHound offers a safe, fun way to find Internet sites related to this book. All of the sites on FactHound have been researched by our staff.

Here's how:
1. Visit *www.facthound.com*
2. Type in this special code **0736854509** for age-appropriate sites. Or enter a search word related to this book for a more general search.
3. Click on the **Fetch It** button.

FactHound will fetch the best sites for you!

INDEX